the
Author's
Walk

Dr. Judith Briles

the Author's Walk

Finding and Using Your Voice to Create Publishing Success

To Rebecca Finkel …

Who continues to awestruck me
with her uncanny ability to bring a book alive
on the cover and on the pages within it,

and

To all writers and authors
who choose to control their author,
publishing, and writing destinies.

MileHigh Press

Mile High Press, Ltd.
www.MileHighPress.com
MileHighPress@aol.com
303-885-4460

The Author's Walk
Finding and Using Your Voice to Create Publishing Success

Books may be purchased in quantity
by contacting the publisher directly or by calling 303-885-4460.
Mile High Press, Ltd.
8122 South Quatar Circle
Aurora, Colorado 80016

Editing: Peggie Ireland, Barb Wilson
Cover and Interior Design: Rebecca Finkel, F+P Design

ISBN Ingram Spark: 978-1-885331-00-7
ISBN eBook: 978-1-885331-01-4
ISBN audio book: 978-1-885331-02-1

LCCN: 2023903239

Writing-Publishing | Aspiring Authors | Reference

Contents

Other Books by Judith... ix

My Author's Note 1

one Listen. Feel. Visualize. 5

two Your Walk Begins 7

three Bringing Juice to Your Writing................. 17

four Growing Your Thoughts and Voice........... 29

five Your Walk Will Have Distractions............. 41

six Why Do You Write?............................ 47

seven Who's Your WHO?............................. 55

eight Your Time Is Everything ...
Finding and Embracing It...................... 63

nine Celebrating Your Muse and Strategy 73

ten Yin, Yang, Fear, Rejection,
and Vulnerability................................ 81

eleven Bringing You and Your Book to Done......... 91

twelve Continuing Your Walk......................... 101

Viva Voce... 109

About Judith.. 111

I'm Grateful... 115

Other Books by Dr. Judith Briles

The Author's Walk

When God Says NO: Revealing the YES

How to Create a Million Dollar Speech

*How to Create Snappy Sassy Salty Success
for Authors and Writers*

How to Avoid Book Publishing Blunders

*How to Create a Crowdfunding Campaign
for Authors and Writers*

AuthorYOU

Show Me About Book Publishing

Stabotage

Zapping Conflict in the Health Care Workplace

Stop Stabbing Yourself in the Back

*The Confidence Factor
Cosmic Gooses Lay Golden Eggs*

*Woman to Woman 2000
Becoming Sabotage Savvy in the New Millennium*

*Woman to Woman: From Sabotage to Support
Smart Money Moves for Kids*

The Briles Report on Women in Healthcare

10 Smart Money Moves for Women

The Dollars and Sense of Divorce

GenderTraps

The Confidence Factor
How Self-Esteem Can Change Your Life

Money Sense

Financial Savvy for Women
The Money $ense Guidebook

Raising Money-Wise Kids

Judith Briles' Money Book

The Workplace

When God Says NO

Woman to Woman
From Sabotage to Support

Faith & $avvy Too!

Money Phases

The Woman's Guide to Financial Savvy

Self-Confidence and Peak Performance

Harmonie Book Series with Brian Barnes

The Secret Journey

The Secret Hamlet

Wake up and think

who ... The **who** is

who you are writing

and publishing for.

What is their pain?

Your words will ease,

soothe, and relieve it.

Now write.

My Author's Note

If your walk is to create
the perfect book, you will fail.

Authors have been in my circle for decades. Clients and friends. Some who have practiced the art of one for the money, two for the show, three to get ready, three to get ready, three to get ready … . Yet they never go.

Chosen stucky-ness. They keep reaching for one more thing; one more piece of information; another interview; another who … knows … what. Their book is in a procrastination quagmire and never gets published. Their quest for the perfect book has become the enemy of creating a good book—even a great book—but their stucky-ness won over.

New authors wait nervously for their first books sales. What will the reviewers say? Will they be picked up by an agent if the goal is to publish with New York? Will they make it to the bestseller list?

Maybe most importantly, will their book sell?

Practice, dedication, and perseverance will have you overcoming the missteps you will no doubt encounter along the way to author and publishing success.

Your writing learning curve can be reduced if you come from a media background such as journalism, film, or even public relations. If you have little writing experience, the curve can be steep and long, but not insurmountable.

The Author's Walk is all about figuring out your path. It will not be a straight one. What walk is straight? You do need to know what your choices are; what the money is all about; how to maximize your time, your energy, and how to create the resources that will support your vision. You need to know who your supporters are and keep the naysayers at a distance.

My caution for you: If your walk is to create the perfect book, you will fail. If you direct your authoring and publishing efforts to creating a good book—even a great book—you will succeed on the Author's Walk. And I'll cheer you on!

Authors should

write about what

they care about ...

always.

one

Listen. Feel. Visualize.

YOUR writing and words will take you places.

> **YOU** *are a writer ... an author-to-be.*
>
> **YOU** *are enough ... you need nothing else.*
>
> **YOUR** *ideas are plentiful ... trust in them.*
>
> **YOUR** *knowledge is abundant ... believe in it.*

Now Start To ...

Listen.

Feel.

Visualize.

and **WRITE** …

Your book is calling to you.

YOUR writing will talk to you.

Welcome its input.

Its inspiration.

Its chaos.

Its truthiness.

YOUR writing and words will take you places.
Places only **YOU**, your creativity, and your imagination
can go.
Welcome them.
Embrace them.

AND ...

    LISTEN to them.

        FEEL them.

            VISUALIZE them.

Your walk. Is ready. To begin.

Now **WRITE** ... your book and readers await **YOU**.

It's the ... **your** ... Author's Walk.

two

Your Walk Begins

As an author, it's your world.
Don't let others lift your sage advice,
ideas, and storylines.

I never intended to write a book.

Unexpectedly pulled to the written word.

If I did not, someone would steal my words away.

Who, and where, would I turn to for help?

I was a reluctant author. An uninvited one. It was a world that I never imagined I would live in or belong to and live in; to see a career that doesn't see an ending to; a world that I came to love and feel great joy as I immersed in it and hung around other authors and publishing providers.

Few knew that I was thinking about writing a book. No one outside of my husband encouraged me to write that first book. A dinner meeting. Someone using and publishing my ideas. An epiphany. And then with a phone call, the ball began rolling.

The only hint of my ultimate vocation as an author and speaker first emerged in elementary school. I talked too much—way too much. I was bored. And I was easily distracted. To stay quiet, I wrote notes to girlfriends and passed them when the teacher's back was turned in my classrooms. Teachers didn't like that. I thought it was normal behavior.

I discovered the power of storytelling on my own. My home had books … but they weren't books the adults in it talked about. They weren't books I was encouraged to read. I was a comic book reader from the get-go—it was how I taught myself to read as a four-year-old when I was at a grocery store with an adult—they always found me there, sitting on the floor reading the latest from the racks. I never knew what compelled me to pull Leon Tolstoy's *War and Peace* one day off the bookshelf in our den. Was it the fat volume? It's hefty weight? The writing on the spine? I don't know. I was nine years old.

What I do know is that it changed my reading life. Devouring page after page, I was mesmerized by this extreme gift of storytelling that unfolded during the turbulent years of the Napoleonic invasion of Russia. All one thousand-plus pages of it. I carried the book around with me like it was my favorite kitten. Every moment I could sneak in, one or two more pages was like a decadent chocolate dessert I'd fallen into.

Then I discovered the power of the library and my first coveted card that opened a vault of riches. Every Saturday, I loaded up my bike basket. Books and the words in them enveloped me. I couldn't stop reading. I was hooked and transported to another world.

It wasn't until decades later when I was the president of a college foundation in Northern California that authoring became a gleam in my eye. A book. Of course, it was to be just one book. I was aware that authors wrote lots of books. But the few authors I knew never did "the tell" … that books breed more books. Oh yes, they do.

But my first book didn't start out as a book idea; it started out as a dinner.

As the president of the foundation, there were perks— I was always included in the private dinner held for our guest lecturers. One time, I volunteered to pick up the speaker in San Francisco, to bring him down to the peninsula where he would speak and I lived.

Walking into the lobby of his hotel, he couldn't be missed. Decked in a Panama hat and white suit was Truman Capote. Heads turned—he loved to be recognized. It was roughly an hour's drive to the presentation site.

Sitting in the front seat, he took in the surroundings of the Bayshore Freeway and spoke. "I've been here before and recognize these hills. I interviewed Perry Smith's sister here." That was a wow for me. His book, *In Cold Blood,*

Truman Capote

was the first true crime I had ever read and is regarded
by critics as the pioneering work in the true crime genre.
I was one of his fans.

He asked me what I did and then asked if he could see
my offices. We did a short redirect when we hit Palo Alto.

As Capote sat at my desk, Money, the live-in office cat
decided she would join me ... and him, plopping in a
long basket on the left side where I typically put papers
for staff to pick up at the end of a workday. She wanted
his admiration as her soft purr emerged. That caught his
eye and ear! Munching on Hershey bar after Hershey
bar, he went on to tell a story that he planned sharing
later to the packed crowd of 3,000-plus at Flint Center
on the college campus. He added another, reading from a
story he wrote as a teen. To this date, it is one of my most
memorable and favorite evenings.

My Mercedes became "the ride" for many authors and
celebrities during my connection with the foundation.
Many I had dinners with.
Others, drinks and hors
d'oeuvres. All were of in-
terest in some way. Many

**Little did I know that his
actions would change my
life and career forward.**

were authors ... some others of note for their expertise
and skill. People like actors Dame Olivia de Havilland

and Cary Grant and photographer Ansel Adams. One of my favorite evenings was with sci-fi writer Ray Bradbury, who to this day, I still quote two lines that he said to me that are embedded in my mind. One dealt with education, the other with immigration:

Ansel Adams

> *It's a dirty trick on yourself if you don't learn and speak English when you come to this country.*

> *My idea of education is that we simply lock all the children up in the library, then open the door when each turns 18 to let them out.*

Ray Bradbury

PASSENGERS
OF THIS LIMOUSINE

Art Buchwald	Gerald R. Ford	Bob Hope
Alvin Toffler	Olivia de Havilland	James Kilpatrick
Truman Capote	Alexander Haig	Gore Vidal
Ray Bradbury	Louis Rukeyser	Patricia Neal
Carl Sagan	Herb Caen	Andy Rooney

*They are schooled and now need to apply it
and live.*

It was a hoot when the head of the program who booked
these awesome men and women presented me with a
plaque that listed all those who had set a foot and tush in
my car—who we affectionately called Ruby.

One evening, my dinner companion was our speaker and
a well-known humorist and columnist. We had a lovely
time; laughing and commiserating about each having
three teenagers and the challenges teens could present.

Little did I know that he was actively listening, chalking
up a slew of ideas that I shared ... and most likely writing
them down after the event in his hotel room or on a pad
on the flight back to New York.

Little did I know that he would turn them into a column based on our dinner conversation within days.

Little did I know that his actions would change my life and career forward.

A week later, I was working in Mexico. Picking up a copy of the *Los Angeles Times*, I came across my dinner companion's column, loaded with *all* my ideas around raising teenagers that I had shared with him. Oh, the column was amusing, but I wasn't feeling so amused. In fact, I was pissed—he never asked permission or even told me he was thinking about writing about our conversation.

Upon my return, there was a letter thanking me for the evening and telling me (warning me?) that he might use some of our ideas in a future column. It was signed, *Cheers—Art Buchwald.*

Yup … *that* Art Buchwald. The Humorist. The Columnist. The Bestselling Author. The Pulitzer Prize recipient.

Our ideas? Future column? How about past tense?

Yes, the "aha" dropped in—my epiphany. I framed the column and his letter. It was my "cosmic goose." All that ran through my mind was, "If I don't start taking some of my own ideas, others will take them … and make money." That was April of 1979. By November, my first book was written.

In December, my agent called me: "We have a book! … we have a book!" were the words that enthusiastically came over the phone line from Jacques de Spoelberch. "St. Martin's Press has bought it and Hope Dellon will be your editor."

When I called my now-first editor Hope to say hello, she told me, "We will publish your book in June."

I'm thinking, *June!? … OK, I can wait; it's only six months from now.*

Ha! She meant June *1981,* not 1980. "We have editing and rewrites to do over the next 12 months. You also will be working with marketing and publicity." What? I thought I had already turned in a "perfect" book … editing had been done before it was sent to my agent.

How wrong I was. A real editor hadn't had her hands on it yet. How clueless I was to the process of working with a publisher and all the elements and steps in this world called book publishing.

Whew … my Author Walk had begun. And what an education and walk it would be.

Writing too many notes in school and getting caught. Talking too much and being sent home multiple times because I couldn't keep still or quiet. Getting dings on my report cards because I was disruptive with my chatter and note-passing. I didn't and wouldn't follow all the rules. Who would have known that they were precursors to my livelihood: being an author and being a professional speaker.

Now, it's **your** *turn.*
As an author, it's **your world**.

Don't let others lift your sage advice, ideas, and storylines.

Stay focused and just go for it.

What "it" turns out to be may literally morph your world.

Whatever, whoever, why-ever you are driven to being an author and writer, celebrate it. Go with the flow. Know that you will hit plenty of hazards and obstacles in your journey. It's normal.

It's the beginning of The Author's Walk … **yours.**

three

Bringing Juice to Your Writing

Successful authors know
that reading other authors
is a significant factor
in their own success.

LISTEN *to your words … your ideas.*

How do they **FEEL** *when you think or say them?*

VISUALIZE *them within a sentence or paragraph.*

Now start **WRITING**,
trusting your fingers as they flow.

Wouldn't you love to be able to pick up a favorite writing tool or a pen/pencil and hit the yellow pad where you noodle ideas? Your brilliant story or solutions for your how-to book magically flow from your ideas—your fingers and thoughts move together, dancing at warp speed. *I would.*

Could you see yourself opening a blank document on your computer and breezing through the chapter you are thinking about … basically having it write itself and be completed within a short period of time? Truly a *Dang, I'm good* declaration to your day. *Count me in, I would love that kind of day.*

Or, how about structuring a series you've been thinking about for the past six months, but somehow, life got in the way? Finally, moving forward at last. *This would have me doing a Happy Author Dance.*

But … but … BUT … it isn't happening.

Have you had one of those "it isn't happening" experiences? Have you had a "my desk is clear—calendar open and there are no hiccups or obstacles to block my creative waves ..." yet it's just not a flowing day? I have had my share of them. What's happening? Could it be your brain cells have taken a hiatus? Are you pooped, and a cruise or a month at the lake is sounding mighty fine right now?

You may have what I call Author or Writer Fatigue Syndrome. I don't know of an author who hasn't been snagged by it at some time. What you need is some major juice. I so get it.

Often, I ask my authors, "Are you *jucilating*?"

"Jucilating? What is that?" It is the typical response accompanied with a quizzical look on my listeners' faces.

Jucilating
(juc-ul-la-ting)

The art of creating new ideas that intrigue others and cath their eyes and open their ears.

"Yes ... jucilating ... my created word for authors to take a time out to discover the art of reenergizing and refueling ideas, words, stories, and solutions that will catch the eyes and open the ears of theirreaders.

So, are you jucilating? Do you want to embrace the pause for refreshing your author and writer creativity and bringing your writing mojo into play?

If you are feeling a tad overwhelmed … or just plain blocked in going forward, try these tips to get yourself back on track.

1. Take a piece of paper and divide it into four sections. In the upper left, label it **ASAP**—those are the items you need, **really** need to deal with. In the upper right, put **7 Days**—these items you have to address within the next seven days—the order of importance is not relevant. In the lower left, write **30 Days**—these are the items/events you need to tackle within the next month. The last section should be labeled **Future.** There's no rush in dealing with any items listed here.

Now, go back to your **ASAP** section—items that need your immediate attention. One option is to cross one or several off the list with a decision that they can't be dealt with immediately and are in the wrong section. All other are to be ignored for now. You are dealing with **ASAP only.** Stay focused—it's so much easier to acknowledge that you can't deal with/do something in the here and now but can address it next week … then let next week arrive. Meanwhile, the **ASAP** list gets whittled down.

2. Review what you've already created/done.

Sometimes just a review will create the goose that can lay your golden egg. That idea that got buried may be stimulated; the scribbly notes you made all of a sudden make sense; or the original idea you had may take on a whole new dimension because you've let it sit in a form of stew for a while.

3. It's gaze-at-the-belly-button time.

What's up? Any thoughts on why you've been stuck or chosen not to go forward with your article, book, work … what? Acknowledge issues preventing you from moving forward. Maybe you don't love the topic or subject any longer. Maybe there's been breaking news or a morphing in the field that has altered your views. Maybe the hero of your story is really a dud.

No matter what, look in the mirror and have a chat with yourself. One of my favorite Keepers is—*Don't do well what you have no business doing.* If what you are working on has become sour … your own … stop it. It's not fun any longer.

4. Review your game plan and goals. Did you ever have any?

That's part of the gaze-at-the-belly-button time. Good idea to start here. Goal setting and game planning can get you back in the frame of mind that you initially had when you started your authoring venture. If you didn't do it, stop and do it now. I can get blue in the face, reminding you that you've got to have the Vision for what you are doing, coupled with the Passion for the project and the Commitment to see it through. When you do run into a hiccup, you've set up the game plan that got you started in the first place. Then it's much easier to cross over the hurdles that pop up.

5. Plan a reward for yourself.

I'm the first to admit it—I've been known to start here. Okay … if I finish this chapter, I get an entire bag of M & Ms—a big one … and I've done that, many times. You've heard of "baby fat"? This is "book fat"! If I finish this book … I get an entire month off of reading any business books and I get to read trashy novels—murder mysteries for 30 days in a row. Hot spit!

- When the first draft is done, I'm going skiing …

- When this section is sent to the editor, I'm watching all the Oscar® winners.

- When I complete this article, I'm …

- When I finish this, I'm booking a cruise to a warm place …

You get the picture. Rewards work. So do incentives. Everyone has different ones that they march to. Find yours. Write them down. And honor them. Just having something you want—even a small Snickers (only one!) or a night of watching reruns of *Seinfeld*, *The Good Wife* , *Breaking Bad* … anything that lets you drop out for a few hours qualifies. It may just be the perk you need to get you back on track or celebrate a job well-done.

6. Escape to the familiar or unfamiliar ... just escape.
I dearly love a great story; yet I don't have the gift of the creative gene that seeds the fiction writer's initial journey —that sometimes wild-ass idea that delivers magic to the eyes of the reader. As a co-author, I can quickly pick up that initial spark and run with it.

Oh, I've worked with many authors who wear the fiction hat—tweaking their words and getting the storylines to flow. I've even had to step in, doing massive rewrites, ghosting a great deal of the book—but the initial idea was generated from the authors. It is their voices … their books.

What I do know is that when I'm stuck and I pick up something else, leaving my "get this finished" work alone for a day or two, it's amazing how my own creative juices can salivate with ideas that get kick-started with some-thing totally unrelated. Kind of like taking a shower and all of a sudden, the "aha" dropping in as the hot water pounds on your shoulders and your stucky-ness goes down the drain.

The "something else" can be fiction … it can be non-fiction … it can be related to your specific genre. The trick is to let another voice come in … think of it as a muse swirling around you … waiting to be invited into your mind and expressed through your fingertips.

Successful authors know that reading other authors is a significant factor in their own success. They devour the way other authors use words and phrases; the style of writing; how a story is set up; what the opening page delivers; how a hidden secret is revealed; and much more. Are you?

7. Know what your writing environment is.

I'm always amused when I listen to an interview with an author who proclaims that getting up at four every morning and writing for four straight hours is the way to be a successful author. Really? It sure isn't mine. Not that I'm averse to getting up at 4 a.m. if that's what the body is saying to do. What I rebel against is someone else telling me how I should write—the time frames, the place, the anything. Coffee bars aren't my thing, either—although I have many clients who thrive in that atmosphere—and I encourage them to go there … often.

I'm a binge writer—have always been; most likely, will always be one. I spend days, weeks, even months discussing it in my head; gathering tidbits of info that I've dropped into a "just in case" file or an expandable file that is actually split up in chapters that will be in the "book."

When my writing mojo is at my side—it's fast, furious, and usually on target. I can bang out a first draft of a book in a short period of time. Recently, I created and taped the entire audio program ... from scratch ... in two days for the new audio and workbook series to augment my book, *Author YOU: Creating and Building Your Author and Book Platforms.* Granted, my butt was a tad sore because I was on the rug in my office, with papers spread around, mic in hand, voice ready. When completed, the tapes were overnighted to the editor. I headed for a cruise four days later.

No one ... and I mean no one ... is/was allowed in my private office space when I move into that writing mode—it's as if there is a yellow crime scene tape across the French doors to my space. Music is on in the background ... my "reward" is close by and my fingers are ready. When I come out to take a health break, get a cup of tea, I check in with staff if my input is needed anywhere. Otherwise, I'm viewed as "out of sight, out of mind" to all.

Authors and writers have habits ... find the ones that work for you, not someone else. Tell those who come into your space your "rules," your "habits"—and that includes the kids. Too many times, when you are at work, you may be the only one that understands that—you are at work. Education is in order. The Author and Writer Fatigue Syndrome is in the shadows.

The journey to and through authordom is long and loaded with detours and hiccups. And that's just creating the book or your article. The journey that you will go on to support the book has even more.

Take care of yourself. Take care of your book. It's Jucilating time. And do think about that cruise!

When you write
from the heart,
you tell the truth.
You connect with
the reader. It's a
good thing.

four

Growing Your Thoughts and Voice

My Author's Walk was finding its mojo.

Do you have a story sizzling inside you?

Or an idea, concept, or solution you want to shout-out?

The question of the moment arises ...

How badly do you want to become an author?

Do you feel the desire really bad ... deep in your bones?

What are you willing to forego to make it happen ...

to see it told ... to see your words in print?

You have thoughts. Ideas for blogs, articles, stories, and topics for your book come in currents ... sometimes even riptides, jerking you in a direction you didn't know you would land in. It happens.

I've ridden countless waves in the discovery process of my words over my forty-plus years of publishing. Waves that cascaded and pounded, and others that were mere ripples. None that I imagined when the idea of publishing a book dropped onto my radar screen.

For me, there was always an idea. Where it worked was when I remained open, allowing for any twists and turns that dropped in. What didn't work was when I meticulously outlined all the details to be included and myopically stuck to them—blocking diversions that could open new paths.

When you grow your thoughts, your voice follows. It may alter it … and strengthen as you continue walking in your authoring path.

My Author's Walk began with an epiphany … *if you don't share your words with others, others will take them and put their name on them.* And they did. A wake-up call was revealed. Would I heed it? I had an idea and solutions I wanted to share … to shout out. *Do you?*

The question rose … Did I want to be an author? My answer was, Yes, I did. *Do you?*

How badly did I want it? Badly enough that I was willing to pay for help. *Do you … would you?*

Did I really feel it in my bones? Yes, again—I started to *see* a book with my name on it. I felt a smile spread across my face as I wrote the words: *a book with my name on it. Do you?*

What was I willing to forego to make it happen … to see it told … and see my words in print? Extra time, my energy on a redirect, and money. I've never regretted it. *And you … what are you willing to forego, to give up on to make your Author Walk come true?*

> *Do you need to go back to school to get a degree in creative writing? Nope.*

> *Do you need an MFA degree … a Masters in Fine Arts, to get your foot in the door? Nope again.*

What you need to do is write … and write lots. Get started. The more you write, the better you write. The better you write, the faster you write. It's my truthiness along with the fact that I know of very few begin-ning authors-to-be who can fork over the $25,000 to $75,000 to add MFA behind their name.

The walk has countless feet to accompany you.

Does it make sense to take writing workshops and attend writing conferences? Yes. And read (and reread as a refresher as your walk continues) William Zinsser's *On*

Writing Well, William Strunk's and E. B. White's *Elements of Style*, Stephen King's *On Writing*, and Anne Lamott's *Bird By Bird*. Excellent words of wisdom and education, all for under one hundred dollars.

And it makes total sense to hang out with other authors … not just newbies. Those who have been through the wringer of publishing. Who get it … and get what you are doing. The walk has countless feet to accompany you.

I knew nothing about structuring a book. Absolutely zilch. My book coach was a novelist and showed up with a tape recorder and told me to start talking. That I could do. Phil said, "I want to hear your voice as you tell your stories to support the concepts we are writing about. Don't worry about hesitating or making mistakes—it will be cleaned up later."

I wanted what I said into the magic machine to be perfect. "Don't worry about being perfect," Phil said. "Just get your ideas out. You know your stuff."

I trusted him and we worked together for six months. I had my notes, a workbook I had created for a class I taught, so I had my material. And I have my words … and my voice. Phil had his tape recorder and my words began to flow. After each session, he would transcribe

them and start the rewrites. It all came back to me ...
then it was my turn to add my rewrites. Back and forth—
we met, I spoke, he transcribed. My speaker mode was
transitioned to learning how to become a writer.

And I did know my "stuff" ... my content. I don't write
and publish on matters I haven't walked. What you as the
author-to-be need to also know—your stuff. As an author,
content is the beginning—
whether it's the story that
weaves through fiction or

**Trust that your discovery
process will reveal itself.**

the solutions, the how-to, or the concepts within nonfiction that are delivered. Without content, there is nothing.
But content can be boring. Ugly boring.

The way you deliver it is where the voice reigns. Yours. It
either sings or falls flat.

When we finished, Phil said, "You have a book. I'm
going to show it to my agent and recommend that he
represent you."

In June of 1981, St. Martin's Press published *The Woman's
Guide to Financial Savvy*. Within a month, it had three
printings. A happy dance time for author and publisher.
Little did I grasp that I had created a walk that was open-
ended.

As I began to write, changes were made. There is a vast difference between our speaking, reading, and writing vocabularies. Data shows that the average adult speaker taps into approximately 20,000 words. The passive reader/writer doubles that number. My mind and fingers had a lot more to say than what flowed from my mouth. The pencil on my yellow pad couldn't fly fast enough across the paper. The year was 1979, long before computers and laptops were the norm at every station in an office.

My yellow pads filled with my *thinking* words. I was on a roll. My secretary Louie said, "JB, there has got to be a better way for you to write."

"Louie, I need to feel my words—this is the way I write."

"Well ... I'm tired of feeling and rewriting your words," was her response.

I was wedded to my yellow pad. Louie was just as wedded to moving on to getting her hands on a word processor.

Caving in, one was leased for three months. I knew that Louie would tire quickly of the new gadget. She didn't.

Louie was a hang glider. Her long-planned two-week vacation was about to commence. Leaving me instructions on how to "boot up" her now-favored tool if necessary, I assured her there was no need—my yellow pad and her IBM Selectric with the interchangeable font balls and correction tape was all I needed. I thought it was the cat's meow.

I was the only one in my office early on Monday morning when my agent called. Mel needed changes on a manuscript he was submitting to New York publishers for bidding consideration. "Make the changes and airmail a new manuscript back to me as soon as possible," I was told.

Oops … the manuscript was stored within Louie's word processor.   **Your file is gone.**

Reading Louie's detailed booting instructions for the third time, I sat in front of my nemesis and followed the first step. It was powered up. So far, so good. The instructions told me how to search for files. I found the one I wanted … and within 30 seconds, I deleted the entire thing. All … of … it.

"Shit!" I shouted out to my empty offices.

Staring at the damn thing, tears flowed. Then I called hubby John who taught engineering and physics at a college. *He's got smart kids … maybe they can fix this …* was my thought. John sent three of them over.

After several hours, it was a no. "Your file is gone."

There were no flash drives or a thing called backup for a small office, FedEx, or the Internet back then. I called Mel. "Airmail my manuscript back to me. I've screwed up and accidentally erased it from the processor. I'll retype and get it back to you by the end of the week."

It was time to put on my Big Girl pants. One of my other secretaries rescheduled all my appointments for the next three days. I would learn how to use the damn thing. Within an hour of commencing my quest, the tears were gone. This gadget was awesome for a writer. Copy. Cut. Paste. **SAVE.**

What a week it was. I typed like crazy and got the manuscript back in the mail, certified delivery. A tech evangelist was birthed. The next stage needed to happen.

I called one of my clients at Apple and asked for consulting help. "Is there a possibility that you can come by my offices and give me some ideas on how to modernize it?"

Forward I went, another step in my Author's Walk.

Owen was the designer for the printer to network the Mac. He could be there at the end of the day. By the next day, five Macs were ordered and delivered by the end of the week.

My staff was thrilled. Louie was stunned when she returned from her vacation.

By 1985, my office was fully computerized, with the last of the IBM Selectrics finding new homes, and being carted with a $200 check to me (versus the $1200 I paid out two years prior). They had become dinosaurs in a short period of time.

A new dawn, a new day, and a new life for me and my writing arrived when I erased my entire manuscript of what was to be one of my pioneering books for women in the workplace. Forward I went, another step in my Author's Walk.

Your author's voice consists of everything from tone to word selection. Using snappy, sassy, and sometimes salty adjectives can set the stage for attitude and mood. Even the punctuation you use is critical and can become part of your writing persona. Your unique use of words, phrases, and style can set your writing and storytelling apart.

For example, you could write about an excursion to the seaside.

My Author's Walk was finding its mojo.

You could focus on the warmth of the sun, the wind whipping up waves, the wisps of hair swirling around the face of your character. Another author could be at the same seaside, yet ignore the waves. He writes about the physical prowess of the surfers' bodies and a variety of other characteristics they physically possess. I suspect that their robust and glistening tan bodies may enter the narrative as well. It's the difference in points of view of every writer's view that creates contrasts between descriptions.

The difference. Some are recognized by fans. Sometimes authors can't hide. One outed Stephen King's pseudonym of Richard Bachman by doing a comparison of a well-known King title with a new one by Bachman. Busted, he was. Your differences are what sets you apart from other authors in your genre.

My Author's Walk was finding its mojo. I began to trust that whatever my discovery process was to be would reveal itself. My voice had come alive on paper—a variation of the speaker voice used on stage. Often with surprises. Be open and let it happen. One of my editors said, "You are a punchy writer." It made me smile when I heard her words. I liked it... punchy was part of my voice!

When I transitioned to keyboard writing, my words expanded. Don't be afraid to just dump out your ideas and then clean them up later. Your brain is in action. Your thoughts are bouncing around. Let them play. Have fun.

I have found that when I pay attention to my voice and allow it to take me in whatever direction it wants to go, words and phrases I meant to use sometimes get mixed up. Something that can rattle a newbie author or someone with a desire to be a perfectionist. Breathe. Let it go … it gets sorted out when you put on your self-editing hat.

Pay attention to your self-editing process—something that I don't dive into until a full chapter is completed—or later. Otherwise, at least for me, I will be tweaking what I have to death. Let it flow. Trust your writing. This is where you make sure your voice … your feelings and nuances can be experienced by your readers. You as the author, are the first round … it's your self-editing process you put in play before you turn your work over to an outside editor.

I was a professional speaker before I wrote my first book. Then, I become one who was writing a book. No big deal. I am now a bestselling, multi-award winning author who speaks about her books. My speaking sold over a million copies of my books. And that is a big deal.

Who are you? What do you want to be?

If you have a message and you believe the world needs to hear it, how important is it to you to get your message out?

What is holding you back? Could it be *you*?

five

Your Walk
Will Have Distractions

Few want to start a walk blindfolded.

The siren of the internet.

Gizmos and gadgets.

Emails. Texts. Life.

Distractions and excuses surround the writer.

Do you know your limitations?

Your Author's Walk starts with a path that your first step is touched upon. If you are thinking writing, authoring, and publishing are a journey, I suggest you rethink it a tad … modify it. Journeys have a beginning and an end. For me, it's aways been a path that led to the full walk. A continual one. I just didn't realize I had stepped on it.

Nor did I comprehend that first step I took was a walk that had no foreseeable end to it. Sometimes short; other times it became a mesmerizing infinity pool of wonder as my words bubbled up; as I eventually published; as I met with fans and readers; as I spoke to groups; and as I was featured on various media channels. All my activities generated ideas for new books. An infinity pool existed that I didn't know was there. The writing world was beckoning to me.

This path and walk weren't truly planned out. There were times that only the goal was in mind—the book … write it, finish it and publish. I have never thought of what I started on as a journey—a verb implying travel. Mine was a task—a noun. Do "it" and get it done and out of my way. And dealing with my "next task."

You will hear a common reference to "the journey" for your writing, authoring, and publishing quest. But is it a journey? *It suggests some form of travel from one place to another* … a day's journey … a journey that took three weeks. Journey can also *mean* traveling a long distance and often in dangerous or difficult circumstances.

Oh, writing can take you on a mind trip or a physical one where you do research on your topic; even traveling to a site for an interview. Could the writing/authoring/ publishing experiences where you travel from one place to another put you in danger? Rarely. Walks can be meandering, open-ended—usually advanced with one foot on the ground while the other is lifted to move forward in a step-by-step process.

That made more sense to me. Not a mishmash of con- fusion … at least I could see ahead what the next step would be. Few want to start a walk blindfolded.

Distractions and excuses. There's a lot not to love here. Yup, there's the internet—a biggie to get you offtrack. And the instant messages and emails that slither in and out through your day. Let's hear it for all the gizmos and gadgets that beckon for your attention—some of them are useful, but many are time-wasters. Not to mention the mindless games that breed on your mobile. And the kids—yes, parenting is essential, and kiddos need to be fed. And the ….

Distractors procreate readily.

The list is endless. It could be a sabotage. Sometimes inflicted by others. Sometimes by outsiders you let in. Sometimes by you, or your mobile, or the tube.

When you are in the writing process, the word *no* needs to become active. You will need to say no to having coffee with others outside of work. Even lunches, shopping. What else?

The coffee thing is a button pusher for me. I get phone calls, emails, and now texts from people I've never heard of ... or barely know, asking, "Can we get together for coffee?"

Ninety percent of the time, my answer is, "I don't drink coffee."

It could be followed with, "How about lunch?"

A variation of my coffee turndown becomes, "I don't have three free hours to be away from my office."

Both are truisms. I don't drink coffee and I work long days. Now, could a close friend call me and ask if I could slip away for a bite to eat? Yes, if I have the window. Likely, I would say, "Come over, I'll have lunch ready." But it's rare—I run a tight calendar. Usually, the people I have no personal connection with simply want to pick my brain (for free) or sell me something!

I may offer a short phone call. I have often said, you are welcome to come by my office and coffee and tea are always ready.

There are two "keepers" I tell all my clients to write down and embrace, both involving a no.

If you never say NO, your YESES are worthless.
Don't do well what you have NO business doing.

And now you have them. You are on a mission, your Author's Walk. Some things need to be pushed back.

Have you ever been pulled away from something you thought was essential to finish? It could be writing a chapter, outlining a new book … it could be something else. But you are at the center and your creative brain has been sparked—a nifty new idea has bubbled up—and you are sidetracked. I know this one well. More times than not, I've good intentions to work on something and an idea pops into my head for a blog. I do two every week … surely, I can whip this up and get back to my good intention. But then a client calls; and then it's time for a scheduled writing session with another client; and then …

In 1972, animator and cartoonist Walt Kelly created the line in his Pogo strip, "We have met the enemy and the enemy is us." You can't escape yourself or them. You can, though, control how you respond when they interrupt you. Being highjacked or held hostage with your time and creativity is not funny.

For we authors, distractions are the enemy of the creative mind. Can new ideas—good ideas—flow when they occur? Sure. And heck, letting your mind do a turn on, tune in, and drop out fantasy/what if time could be exactly what you need to jucilate.

Just be aware ... they can also sabotage you finishing what you are on track to do.

Grab your walking stick and don't let the distractions blur your focus and redirect you. I promise you ... they will.

six

Why Do You Write?

Go to it, embrace it,
magnify it, fill your writer sphere
with its sensations.

> *Someone.*
> *Something.*
> *Event.*
> *Happening.*
> *Trigger.*
> *Reaction.*
> *It's the* **WHY** *you write.*

Do you have a favorite piece of music or a song? For me, when I hear the opening measures of Rachmaninoff's *Rhapsody on a Theme of Paganini, Op. 43*, anticipation surfaces. It's my favorite piece of classical music. I settle in with my hands wrapped around a mug of tea and lean my head back, closing my eyes. I'm waiting for the flow of glorious notes that I think is all that divine can be. I can savor the pleasure that will soon envelop my ears as it enters this phase of the rhapsody.

Okay, I confess. When I wrote this, I let the distraction gnat in … I just uploaded a version from *YouTube* featuring the Singapore Symphony and Lukas Geniusas at the keyboard so I could savor it one more time and continue to write.

Onward. I'm also jazzed when I hear the cascading buildup to the crescendo of Maurice Ravel's *Boléro*, a beautiful and haunting musical work of art. As it begins, subtlety and softly, with the first tap of the snare drums, then the flute enters, my head is moving affirmatively with the beat that transitions to my toes and then the heel of my foot joins in. The rhythm transcends up and down my body. By the end, I have virtual cymbals. It ends as loudly as every piece in the full orchestra can make it. Immersed I become. Fantastic!

Am I stimulated when I hear them? Yes. Do they inspire me? Absolutely.

Music can quickly capture your energy, focus, and passion (or lack of it) without a lot of thought or work.

Do you have a favorite song?

One that captivates the rhythm of your heart and your message?

What song describes your workplace and the people you work with?

How about your homelife—and just life in general?

Does your writing music flow from your soul and through you as you think about a chapter you are writing ... your book?

Or are you listening, and dancing, to someone else's beat —their rhythm, their song?

Your writing and your forthcoming book carries a part of you—the fabric of your life woven with your experiences, feelings, and beliefs. What does it look like? Feel like?

Why do authors write books? Why does anyone publish them? The reasons are numerous. One of the ways to enhance your status as *the expert* is to write a book. For others, it's their life's work. You could have had an epiphany of some sort or experienced an amazing event or feat. You may be bubbling over with ideas for children's books or the next murder-mystery series.

Who knows how you got here … what you do know is that you have heard the calling. Somewhere inside of you, the author siren is reaching out to your authordom. What book is in you?

We each came to the authoring party using a different route. You are hearing the authoring siren. It's now your turn—your words, experiences, stories, or illustrations and fantasies; your successes in working with specific industries, types of clients—even case studies that may not include names but give hope to someone looking for some help that you understand their industry, situation, or concerns.

Becoming a writer and then an author is usually driven by one word.

All of which your imagination pulls from.

> *Does everyone have a book in them? No. The simple truth is that there are too many mediocre books—from cover and interior layout design to being content-awful—that are created and published every year. Your book should not only be good, but look good. And read well. A standout in the crowded and polluted book world.*

Becoming a writer and then an author is usually driven by one word: *inspiration*. The problem with inspiration is that it is an elusive bugger at times. The other word that supports inspiration is *rhythm* … a blending begins to happen when you are assembling your words.

What the magic cosmic goose is for you may be a total turnoff for another. What brings joy and laughter to you may send a fellow writer into a spiraling downer. That's a bummer when that someone is a friend or writing partner.

But somehow, you got it. The inspiration fairy dusted you, and words and book pages appeared in your eyes and fingers.

The key is to find what works for you. Then go to it, embrace it, magnify it, fill your writer sphere with its sensations—the sounds, odors, visuals, tastes, and touches of the things that bring you calm. Focus on what inspires you; that opens your creative juices; and that allows you to enter into a world that is yours, and yours alone. Welcome the bliss and joy you will experience.

When you are inspired, you can sense and feel your words.

It could be a marathon of silly movies; a garden of spectacular colors blooming; the surrounding aroma of coffee or holding a hot mug of a favorite tea; the bouquet of a red wine; a walk on the beach; the pounding of the surf or the flow of a waterfall; the joy of hearing little kids laughing; sitting down with friends over a meal and just talking; or belly laughing at an event or movie—my kids actually moved away from me at a movie because I embarrassed them.

How about a deep dive into a favorite book ... cooking up a storm ... puttering in a shop; the wonder of sunrises and sunsets—sunrises especially; the solitude of a gentle rainfall; the serenity of a breaking dawn; the immersion in a lecture ... anything that welcomes the creativity and focus gods into my space.

Hmm, as I wrote this, I felt my head nodding affirmatively. These are many of the things that I love—things that raise my happiness meter. And there's a rhythm and flow within each of these visual scenes I mentioned above. When I'm in the happy zone, inspiration becomes a welcome playmate.

When you are inspired, you can sense and feel your words. The jucilating moment has entered your space —stuff, environment, sights, smells, sounds, flavors, happenings, sensations—all juice that sparks your ideas and ahas.

For the fiction writer, overhearing a patch of a conversation sitting in a theater, coffee shop, or the airport may seed an amazing dialogue between characters that your imagination hadn't revealed yet—the ones that create a chewy sentence or scene in your writing.

For the nonfiction author, observing and hearing a kaleidoscope of thunder and lightning as it dances across the sky could unravel the string of descriptive metaphors you've been seeking. I love it when that happens.

It's critical to know where your creative juices come from; to know what your sources are that jumpstart you for any project that needs your full focus. In today's multi-everything ... from the media, stimulus, and causes worlds, it's easy to get offtrack. The "squirrel factor" pervades. Wham ... in a nanosecond, your attention can be distracted, your body and mind pulled in an entirely different direction. It's as if something—sometimes a someone—is clicking a remote control in your head—pulling you in many directions but not in the direction you thought, or wanted, to go in.

We authors are our own type of warrior and a Warrior Author must know what the driver behind his or her energy is and feed it—the juice ... the inspiration ... and the rhythm.

When nourished, amazing things are accomplished. The book is completed. A workbook to accompany an existing program is produced. A webinar or podcast series is rolled out. The kickoff of a new book project or a book launch is planned and ready to execute. Your possibilities seem endless. And they are.

You may write because it's in you to get your stories out. You may have no intention to publicly publish them … yet. But you are going to get them out. You write because you've been inspired. Your inspiration increases as you get into a rhythm—your rhythm—for writing. It's your new song.

seven

Who's Your WHO?

You want to be the whale in the pond.

> *Readers can be frustrating.*
>
> *Most haven't found you … yet.*
>
> *Seek them.*
>
> *Know them.*
>
> *Go where they are.*
>
> *Nurture them with your words.*
>
> *They are your WHO.*
>
> *You are found.*

Then there's the "WHO" part. Who is your reader? If you think it is the world ... everybody ... do you feel a virtual slap headed your way? That's me. Only a fool would think his or her book is for everyone ... a fool.

That won't be you.

For years, my clients and audiences have heard me say,

> *It's better to be the whale in the pond than the sardine in the sea.*

Another truthiness. It means to know what your niche is.

My friend Joan Stewart, known as the Publicity Hound, would routinely ask every author who we met; every attendee in our zillions of workshops we did together,

> *Tell me what your book is about?*
> *Who is it for?*

Typically, the responses would land in the "F" category if they were to be graded. Only a small number could say what their book was about in two sentences. That would be about one percent. Ugh.

The Who question didn't fare much better. Gag me if I hear the response that has the word *everybody* in it.. Everybody is not your reader. Oh, many start down the reading path devouring whatever comes into it. Soon the selected favorites bubble up.

Think about you—what's the genre that you like to escape to? Or the author whose books you buy automatically—no matter what they write? That author is not writing for everybody—he's writing for those who are looking for mysteries, or thrillers, or sci-fi, or horror, or romance— you name it There's a lane he's writing in for the reader who is waiting for the next book to land in it.

If you are a romance writer, your readers are looking for romance, cozy, feel-good books. Go find them—you want them in your reading corner. That's what superfans are—individuals who devour whatever is new in their favorite genre. Stephen King may have the #1 latest fiction book or there's a hot "tell-all" political bio or memoir out—but if it isn't romance, cozy, woven with good vibes, and have a happy ending, it's a pass. Superfans stay in their lane.

There is an audience for your book.

Think of your favorite restaurants; the ones you frequent. Odds are that you order the same thing. Why? Because it speaks to you and seduces you with flavors you love. You are a superfan of the item, of the restaurant. Count me in here. I have a few I like to go to. Thanking the wait staff for the menu, I study it … and then order what I always do. At one, it's always the crab cakes. At another, the eggplant parmigiana. Are you like me?

The previous chapter was about the **WHY**. I revealed how I loved a few classical music pieces and the inspiration they deliver when I settle in and listen. If there was a local concert featuring either one, tickets would be bought and I would be there.

Here's the secret sauce: There is an audience for your writing … for your book. But you must know who it is. Then you cater to that audience—forget about the others. Write for it. Market to it. And be grateful it exists. These people are your superfans-to-be.

Questions for you to munch on include:

- What is it that readers like about your genre?

- Why are readers enthusiastic about your genre?

- What authors are writing in this genre now?

- Which authors are in the top five on the genre's bestseller list on Amazon?

- What are readers saying about their books on Amazon reviews or Goodreads?

I tell all my clients to imagine their reader. Do this now. Close your computer and look across from where you are.

Your reader is ready to have a mug of tea, cup of coffee, or a glass of wine with you. Nice.

What's his or her name? Start a conversation. Yeah, yeah, I know. If someone was observing you, they might think you are a tad off—but who gives a twiddly-dit … not you. You have moved into essential territory.

Let's say your ideal reader is me. I'm Judith.

What secrets are behind my smile? What about pain or quirks? What about disasters and mistakes? Where have I stumbled and kept it a secret? How about any plans or hopes I might have? What about fun stuff? Are there any movies or binge-watching episodes worth exploring?

Oh boy, we need more tea. Or maybe a little vino.

And here's a tip—having the "conversation" with your ideal reader is a trick I use if I'm feeling stuck on an idea. My mythical fan never responds, but my mind does. The writing moves forward. Some of the dialogue is a hoot.

I can't leave you without finishing my thoughts about Amazon reviews. Read them, especially the one- and two-star reviews. Why? Because the readers tell you where the author missed the writing boat.

And please, be able to say **WHAT** your book is about in two sentences. Your goal is to make your listener want to hear more and ask questions that opens a dialogue.

Got it? You want to be the whale in the pond. Know your reader. Forget about the zillions of sardines in the vast publishing sea—most will be eaten. Know your **WHO** lane.

Let's take another step on your walk.

Writers are like sponges. The more we read the genres we write in, the better we get.

eight

Your Time Is Everything ... Finding and Embracing It

If you are only dabbling, thinking about it,
you haven't crossed the writing bridge yet.

> *To become an author ...*
>
> *To become a **DOER**, not a dreamer ...*
>
> *You gotta write. It's the only way.*
>
> *It's a big step ... that first step.*
>
> *Are you ready to take it?*

So many writers ask me if there is a "rule" for how much they should write a day. As in word count. Hours in. Are there minimums they must meet to succeed? And must they write every day? In my opinion, most ideas like this that have filtered their way are silly and unrealistic. And, in my opinion, the only Rule is to starting writing if you want to be an author. It's a step-by-step forward as you begin your walk.

Phooey to all the "rules" you have heard. Make your own … ones that fit your timeframe, your needs, your families, and for many of YOU, around your day job.

Does your word count matter? Hmm, a good question. In my opinion, nope. Dump it. My question would be: Are you writing … anything? A sentence? A paragraph or two? What about lots … a draft of a chapter … *just something*? That would be a start.

Some say you must write 1,000 words a day. Really? The better question is to look within and see what's flowing. Are you on a writing stream and it's hot, hot, HOT? What do numbers matter? You may drop in a few thousand. Just freaking *write*. If it's a noodle time, then noodle— smoosh the words around and see what starts to gel. It could be only 100 words … but a magnificent 100.

As a writer—I'm writing shorties and longies. It could be blogs, an eblast to my followers, or a complete chapter. Typically, I grind a chapter out rough, then come back to it. Word count is irrelevant to me. Does what I wrote make sense?

If it's nonfiction, is there a beginning, a middle, an end ... and a CTA—call to action? Do I have a lead hook to lure the reader in? If not, I add it. If fiction, are my words moving the storyline forward? Is there too much telling? Does the opening make sense? Does the reader want more to keep turning the pages? Does the end of the book make sense?

If you are only dabbling, thinking about it, you haven't crossed the writing bridge choice yet. Diddling and dabbling doesn't get a book done. Writing does.

Once you cross, then commitment comes into play. You start believing that you will have a book ... become an author. Woo Hoo! The virtual carrot is dangling in front of you. Now is your time to turn your virtual dream into reality.

To become the author you desire to be, it's time to become a **DOER**, not a dreamer.

Do writing hours count? Maybe. I cringe when I hear someone say that you gotta get up at 4 a.m. and write until 6 or 7 a.m. ... before the kids awake, or work demands you show up. Or in the still of the night, when all are asleep, the time is all yours. Maybe. Is 4 a.m. a good time for you? Are you a creative at the crack of dawn or are you a night owl? Best to know where your best jucilating time is. Words come to writers at oddball times.

For writers with a sizzling desire to become an author, it's a prioritizing time. What's important to you … as in the top four. Spouse? Kids? Day job? Care of an elder? What?

We all have lists of important stuff in
Short is the new black.
our lives. What are yours? If taking a few weeks to just have "us time" with your spouse … you do it. If being at the kids' events is up there, you do it. If making sure you are spending time with a friend or relative who is aging is important, then you map it out and do it.

If watching TV on downtime; playing video and mobile games; the lure of gizmos and gadgets have hooked you; the internet; or whatever are not deal breakers in your everyday life balance, then dump them and substitute. That's new book-writing time. Time you thought you didn't have.

Look … we all waste time—all of us, including me. For years, when I would come home from a speaking gig—sometimes having been away for weeks, my John would find me in the kitchen. It was part of my re-rooting back, making something, before I was ready to settle into the other creative mode my work demanded. Did I need to really create a week's worth of meals? Nope—although I've done it. It's back to gazing-at-the-belly-button time. What do you really need to do … must do?

You've got a calendar—get time blocks on it now—color-code so you know what is flexible and what is not. And start calendaring yourself in—When I do, my online calendar blocks the time span with my favorite color, purple. It's automatically labeled as *JB Time*.

Do word counts count?

When you are writing, you get better at it.

Do the hours you put in matter?

And must you write every day?

You are reading this. I'm assuming your goal is to write ... or write more. To become an author ... and a successful one as you define what your personal success is. A finished book needs words in it. It doesn't need 100,000 of them if half the amount reveals what the reader needs or desires. For years, I've said that *short is the new black*. Where 82,000 was a typical nonfiction book in 1981; under 60,000 is fine today.

In fact, under 40,000 is acceptable if the stage/premise is set and the reader gets the author's insights and closure. Heck, even shorter if it works. Time is limited for many. Readers of both fiction and nonfiction love what is called an airplane read—board, buckle up, wheels up, page-turner, land—book finished.

Short is the new black—don't get stuck on your word count. If your book is complex and needs lots of them, don't shortchange your reader. It's your story. It's your ideas. It's your info that counts.

Most likely, what you are currently doing involves writing *every* day. It is for me. As I write this, I have two personal books in the works, plus my fingers in ten others with multiple clients. One of mine is the second book in the Harmonie series, *The Secret Hamlet*. My co-author Brian Barnes and I are at the 40% mark, ready to dive in with our three-times-a-week joint writing sessions.

The other ten are buzzing around—I've shot off short notes to three of them with ideas for them … and then I stopped. They have scheduled time already on my calendar—client time is coded in a fuchsia color with each client's name on their time. Then it's back to *JB Time* on my calendar. Otherwise, I could spend the rest of the morning thinking about other things, which would be distractors.

Do I write a chapter or work on a chapter every day for my own book? Nope. Every week? Nope. How about every month? Maybe—it depends. Oh, I think about it. Write notes to include, stuff not to forget, and slip them into the book's exclusive folder for my later use.

I have lots of writing to do. Blogs, ezines, campaigns for social media every week. Clients' books that I work on daily—and they each have their time slot on my calendar. Sometimes a note to a friend—a quick catchup.

The point is, I'm writing. And that's what is important here. When you are writing, you get better at it. Your mind is moving. Your hands are moving. And your creativity is being fed—even with what seems like mundane writing. When I look back at my writing in my first book published in 1981, compared to my style, verbiage, and punch that I use today—whew ... what a difference.

Yes, I write every day ... lots. And I bet you do more than you think you do—even notes to yourself, your kids, a reminder to someone—all writing. When I decide that today I will work on my book, then the thinking, some of the creativity I needed in posting a podcast I taped earlier in the week could just be the lead for the chapter I will work on. How cool is that? I never know. I take notes during the show—phrases that my guest uses could just be a missing link for something I'm working on.

How do I finish a book? All those notes, reminders, articles, maybe previous blogs I've written could work into it. All gathered in my place awaiting me. And then I'm ready. All of them come together and then I go underground for a week. It's been on my calendar for eight months. A cruise. One intense week of writing. No cooking, no clients, no nothing. Food is available to me when I want it. My favorite iced tea ready. And I write from the time I wake until I'm ready to break—10 to 14 hours each day for six to seven days. When I reappear, I have a draft done. And ready for my self-editing round before handing it off to my editor for her red-ink time.

It's my form of seclusion—no outside noise that I don't choose to have around me is allowed. It's water and sun that I want in my life for my writing intensives. Salt air was something I have in common with Albert Einstein. He revealed,

> On the other hand, although I have a regular
> work schedule, I take time to go for long walks
> on the beach so that I can listen to what is going
> on inside my head. If my work isn't going well,
> I lie down in the middle of a workday and gaze
> at the ceiling while I listen and visualize what
> goes on in my imagination.

It's my way. I need space to listen to my head. Maybe not yours, but it's what's worked for me for many books now. I need to gaze out and visualize "what's next here?"

Find your way, a rhythm that works for you. It could be daily or every evening; an underground weekend twice a month; a getaway for several extended days. The local coffee shop could be your spot. It could be at home or a resort. I have a client who books a hotel room, orders her favorite meals in, and stays there for several days. She does it often—it's her rhythm. Colorado Authors Hall of Famer sci-fi author Kevin J. Anderson gets on his hiking boots, grabs his recorder and heads for the trails. It's the way he writes the first draft of his gazillion books.

To write well, creativity needs to be in play. Nourish yours. Don't worry about word count or how many hours you are at it. Get your calendar out. **YOU TIME** is waiting. Just get started.

nine

Celebrating Your Muse and Strategy

It will inspire you to continue to write
—but to what end?

The muse sprinkles muse dust.

Choice—success or mediocrity?

Strategy is developed.

Your sweet spot identified.

I like the thought of a muse in my midst. Something that drops in for a chat. Okay, it's a chat in my head. A goose. An inspirational nudge. The muse inspires you, ignites your imagination, and thrills you with a paragraph that sings off the page in perfect poetry. Maybe a tad of giddiness surfaces. You love spending time with her—I always think of mine as *her*—she has few boundaries and is always grateful for anything that flows from my hands onto the pages and whatever I'm working on.

For me, she surfaced early when I realized I was more productive in good weather. Some warmth from the sun. And water. A sea breeze or a shimmering lakefront. I am drawn to the movement of the ocean on our annual cruises. Sometimes I have to settle for a poolside or having an outdoor gurgling fountain close by—a soothing sound for me. Even an early morning hot tub soak with a mug of hot tea sets the stage.

My water muse helps me to set goals on myself to "get it done"—whatever the done is to be:

> *The* muse *knows ideas will float out there
> in your imagination, or in piles of journals,
> notes, and files. It will inspire you to continue
> to write—but to what end?*

Musing through your writing space might sound like a brilliant idea. But there's a string attached. What the muse brings to you in your creation or words, ideas, and stories, it often doesn't lay out the organization side of getting your book published. You need a strategy. You have the passion to write. Now you need it expanded to a passion

that sells books and develops the *strategy* that enables
you to connect with your readership and your audience.

Developing a strategy is soul-easing. Creating it points
the way to order. Books need order and organization. So
does what you are writing. Organization is the antithesis
of "the overwhelm."

Mediocre authors who hate to market and sell books don't.

When you identify the strategy
that works for you, it's equivalent
to having the right shoes—the ebb-and-flow of what you
are doing. You become energized—a good thing when
you are writing.

What does all this mean to you—the new author? When
approaching publishing, you will encounter what seems to
be an endless list of things to do. New ideas are probably
bred as you sleep. Author fatigue can set in. Soon, the
overwhelmed feeling pounces and you are buried under
emails, sticky notes, mobile cell phone calls, voicemails,
social media posts—you name it. You are being stretched.

You come up for air, scratching your head and wonder
where your writing is going. And, if you have a book
completed—what happened to it. Personal life, forget it.
Balance and rhythm are long gone. All you feel is out of
step with life, work, and your book.

Your life preserver is threefold: strategy, planning, and priorities. Before you groan, understand that successful authors strategize, plan, and prioritize. Mediocre authors who hate to market and sell books—*don't*. What's your choice—success or mediocrity?

Of course, you desire to be successful. Right?

If you spend all your time, money, and effort without a clear plan, you will find yourself jumping from guru to guru, always looking for the next best thing. You may even become a workshop/conference junkie—looking for the instant solution to getting it all done. In a sense, you become both predator and prey. You seek the magic formula that will take

Saving money is not a bad thing.

you to the best-seller list, whether it is the latest internet strategy or a print-on-demand program that overpromises and underdelivers. You spend your money, but have little to show for it other than boxes of books that you can't sell.

And then you realize you are on your own—the gurus have moved on, along with your money.

If you are a DIY saver—insisting on doing it all your-self—it can cost you untold amounts of money. Often, a DIYer isn't the best person to do the job needed to create the final book. There are many skill sets required to get your book done.

Whether it's laying out one's own book, designing the cover and worst of all—doing a one-stop editing process that only the author does or having an old high school English teacher take on the task, red flags are waving. Any one of these tasks is a potentially huge money-loser … and common characteristics of the DIY author.

Saving money is not a bad thing, but without a solid strategy for how and what to save on, an author could easily end up with a cheap-looking book that ultimately needs rescuing to have any chance of survival. And starting over. The result is more money will be spent to correct their mistakes because they, as the author, took on the wrong tasks. Not to mention the time lost.

Authors should be willing to pay for guidance from people who have more experience than they do. Is that something that would help you? It's the way to increase book sales, reduce costly mistakes, and to avoid kissing off money. My book, *How to Avoid Book Publishing Blunders,* will save you time, energy, and money. It will help you with book design, editing, and marketing tips. If you don't have this title, get it pronto. For added strategies for increasing cash flow and marketing your expertise, add *How to Create a Million Dollar Speech* to your checkout. One will help you red-flag mistakes and get author-smart fast. The other will show you how to make money on your book with what I call the Cash-Cow Two-Step.

You don't want to waste your money or waste your time. Remember that spending money to make money sometimes needs to be done. Hiring a personal assistant a few hours a week takes the long list of to-dos off your plate, leaving you to focus on building your networks, doing book signings, and reaching out to your particular market.

The WHOs that are essential to your author success sweet spot will welcome the muse and integrate all success strategies. With it, balance comes into play.

What about book coaches and book consultants? If they know their stuff—your genre—and have a track record, they can stretch your skills and success quotient. Do your homework. I'm a goal-pushing coach/consultant that is blatant with my advice to my clients. Oh, I hand-hold, encourage, and have fun with them. But the goal is to get the book done. Know what your own goal is before you step into the water.

When you ...

- *Spend time* learning;

- *Spend money* on new tools;

- *Save money* by sticking to your plan, picking the best people to help you publish your book;

- *Invest in help* you need to learn a whole new skill set; and

- *Move* forward with the constantly changing world of publishing ...

Author success comes into your midst.

It's the muse and strategy working together. The sweet spot for your triumph over those who want to write a book and never do.

ten

Yin, Yang, Fear, Rejection, and Vulnerability

What you write is for your readers.

The Who. Never forget it.

You are published.

Nakedness.

The trolls await you.

A one-star review.

A rejection.

Deep breath time.

Persistence.

Is everyone going to love what you write? What you publish? Who are you kidding … of course they aren't. As an author, it's wise to know that at times, a thick hide needs to surface. There will be critics. Sometimes legitimate. Sometimes there will be ones that you will put in the major jerk category—okay, asses.

Once your work is published, the vulnerability factor surfaces. You are exposed. Naked. Friends will support you. Fans will discover you.

None rejected me or my manuscript with the standard boiler-plated rejection letter.

And then there are Foes. Oh, there are a few … and they can sting and zap the best of us. The trolls of the universe. They seem to pop up in book reviews like a swarm of irritating gnats.

Every author I know has been dumped on at some time. Reviews can be truthful … and wrenching. If there are multiples grumbling about editing, context, storylines that disconnect, authors better go back to what they wrote. Revisit it. Their book might be loaded with errors and the dings are warranted. Fix them and upload new files pronto if you can.

One of my most successful books was *Woman to Woman: From Sabotage to Support*. At the time, the William Morris

Agency represented my work. Every major publisher
rejected the proposal and manuscript—every one of them.
None rejected me or my manuscript with the standard
boiler-plated rejection letter. One took her time to jab
me with all that was wrong including a detailed letter
that said that it would be impossible to get any media
coverage—the topic was so toxic and erroneous. And so
… so … much more was thrown at me. Rejection wove
through my body.

I knew in my heart of hearts that it was a breakout book.
A pioneering book. A buzzed-about book. But not per
the big boys—who were actually all women editors—in
New York. Rejected it was. I ended up signing with an
independent third tier publisher. "This is an important
book," was what the new editor said. "It needs to be
out there … blah … blah … blah." I signed, knowing
my book was all those things. And I was ignorant—so
ignorant about what I had gotten into. I knew nothing
about independent publishing, thinking that legit
publishing came only via New York.

Woman to Woman came out. Eight printings. Cover story
in *People* magazine. *Oprah* called. The *Wall Street Journal*
called, as did the *National Enquirer*. The *Chicago Tribune*
named it the Business Book of the Year. Over 1,000 media
interviews. Ha … and so there to rejection!

My 28 rejections were nothing compared to the 750 rejections collected by sci-fi master author Kevin J. Anderson who also earned the trophy for *The Writer with No Future*. With 175 titles under his belt as I write this (think *Star Wars*, *X-Files*, and *Dune* universes), he has sold 23 million books. You might want to grab his book, *Slushpile Memories: How NOT to Get Rejected*.

So ... what's the secret sauce to publishing? One word: persistence.

In the beginning of *The Author's Walk*, I asked the *Why* question. Revisit it:

> *Why are you writing? Your Why may be Whys and are numerous. One of the ways to enhance your status as the expert in a field. Or it's your life's work? You could have had an epiphany of some sort; experienced an amazing event, or feat; you may be bubbling over with ideas for children's books or the next murder-mystery series.*

Who knows ... they may be numerous ... but you got here. What you do know, is that you have heard the calling. Somehow, the author and publishing sirens beckoned to you.

Your book carries a part of you—the fabric of your life woven with your experiences, feelings, and beliefs.

What does your book *look* like?

What does your book *feel* like?

Does your book title have an *emotional* hook to it?

If it doesn't have a title yet, let's get a "working" one in play. Know that titles often morph as writing continues. Many times, I've been firm on it long before I started writing—just knowing that a new book was beginning to form in my head. At others, I've changed it days before going to the printer ... something that my layout designer wasn't thrilled about.

What does book success look like for you?

Authors come to the authoring party using a different route. You have RSVP'd to the invitation.

It's now your turn. You've heard the call. What will you do with the song that weaves through your head?

Having a book, with your name on it as the author adds a significant notch in the credibility game. It goes beyond just a business card; it becomes part of your heart and soul. I have never been in a gathering of people where someone doesn't say, "I've been told that I should write a book about ..." or "I want to write a book ..." or "I'm thinking of writing a book ..." Getting that book out takes curiosity; it takes courage; it takes creativity; and it takes commitment. Lots of each.

Successful authors usually start by looking in the mirror. Do it. Ask yourself before you start your walk:

- What inspires you—people and places?

- What separates you from other authors?

- What are you an expert in?

- What path led you to create this book?

- How will you write your book?

- How will you learn about your publishing options?

- People can drain you. How will you deal with others when you want to ... need to ... write?

- What assistance will you need to write your book?

- What do you need to publish your book?

- What does book success look like for you?

In Joseph Campbell's book, *The Power of Myth*, he declares:

Follow your bliss and the doors of the universe will open to you.

That would be a shout-out **YES** to me. **GO FOR IT.** The "it" comes through loud and clear when I read his words. The beginning steps that you've taken so far have led to the moment where you can declare:

- Who you are as an author.

- What your book is about.

To the doors of the publishing universe, you are saying hello. The arms of bliss await you. As you developed your statements for your book, think about the patterns you are creating. Who you want to portray.

- Are they consistent with who you are?

- Are they consistent with the book you want to deliver?

Are there any hiccups that show that you could be wasting time or running in circles—hiccups that might act as a barrier in your authoring journey?

With books, you need to tune into your message or storyline. Listen to what your "audience" says it needs/wants. Reflection, evaluation, and connection are the genesis with what your book is about.

Think of the concepts of Yin and Yang. Yin is all about emotion. With emotion comes the passion for "why" your book is in creation.

It's the Yang that will make it happen. The intricacies that you are challenged with as you expand the ideas and concepts that originally seeded the idea. Be it fiction or nonfiction, this is where the basic steps are critically coupled with the glitzy ones. It's the shine you bring to your authoring pen. This is not where you want to spin your wheels—adding fluff when it's not necessary or diverting from your core.

As a writer, your goal is to have others enjoy what you write. What you publish. You don't write for reviewers. Or for good reviews. You will get them. You will get some so-so ones. Once you have explored what many similar grumbles are and determined that you are standing behind what you published, let it go. If the grumbles are about poor editing and typos galore, get them fixed.

What I've learned with my years of being vulnerable is that some of those "so-so" comments come from envy. You wrote the book; you published—and the reviewer didn't.

What you write is for your readers. Your Who. Never forget it.

Rejection is never
fun. Stay focused;
stay the course,
work hard and
honor your voice.
A **yes** is coming!

eleven

Bringing You and Your Book to *the* Done

This is the rhythm in an Author's Walk that leads to results.

> *Fear.*
>
> *Doubt.*
>
> *Write.*
>
> *Content.*
>
> *Story.*
>
> *Rewrites.*
>
> *Done.*
>
> *Your Book.*

Writers and publishers experience much the same. You are taking your inner voice out into the world stage, nervously wondering how you will be judged. You feel like you are buck naked with all eyes directed toward you and your words. Entering into the unknown world requires you to be willing to look foolish as you begin your walk and the often overwhelming steps to your coming success. Don't expect to sit down, write for 90 days, and generate an instant blockbuster.

Colorado Authors' Hall of Famer Stephen King creates blockbusters. His success didn't happen quickly. And it didn't happen overnight. He honed his craft, read upwards of 80 books a year, and practiced, practiced, and practiced his writing. His was a talent in development. It was not one that appeared to him in an instant. He found the grace in a sentence well written. He developed a routine which worked well for him—writing every day, mostly in the morning.

King thought he needed a huge desk to continue his success. It was cumbersome and he got rid of it. In its replacement was a simple desk and comfortable furniture —a place where his kids could visit him, share a movie and a pizza when he took a break from writing.

> *Stephen King learned from other authors,*
> *developed friendships with many of them he*

*respected—seeing them more as collaborators,
compatriots on a similar journey—not his
competitors.*

And he focused on the basics. And the fundamentals:
vocabulary, grammar, the elements of style. Acknowledging
that some bad writers might become competent writers;
some good writers will become great writers; and some
writers will fail to make the cut for various reasons. His
book titled *On Writing* is one that I recommend to all
authors—aspiring and already published. It's not to be
read only once. Revisit it as you would a reliable friend.

Publishing your book requires the fundamentals of a
well-crafted book: title, cover, editing, layout, and printing.
Marketing and selling your book—the basics start with
telling people you are writing a book—each and every day.
And then promoting and marketing once it's available for
sale. Let those you've already shouted out to—they are
missing something very important if they don't read it.

Writers need to write. Some days are spent on your book.
Others could be blogging or articles. Writing. Each day
in a writer's life is awakened by the call. Publishers need
to sell books. Writing and publishing your book can be
fun and rewarding. It will take dedication—lots of it. It's
work. Taking a few scattered words—extending them

into an image that sends you to the next sentence and beyond becomes the rhythm in your Author's Walk.

The same rhythm on your walk leads to results. Taking you on a heartfelt experience, one that you may not have anticipated. The rhythm of the pen, the click of the computer keys are the steps that take you on this marvelous and often frustrating path toward your first sentences. Sentences that are surprisingly good and that take you—the author—down a subconscious passageway wondering—where did that come from?

It's a jucilating moment. And it might become some of your best writing.

The highs of the perfect paragraph can be followed with the lows of bloopers and blunders. All of it awaits you.

It is the learning from your mistakes, malfunctions, and the like that fuels action—not just motion. Just as in your storytelling, whether fiction or fact—you need to move the story along. We all want to, *need* to solve problems, and overcome conflict—it is the passion of life to do so. And so must you ... for your-self ... and for your readers.

Your book starts in the incubator of your mind.

Your technique is important. Essential.

Too often, authors think they will get through their first draft, clap their hands together in joyous celebration, thinking they are finished and will have a book out in the next month or two. Then, they see the red lines and comments from the editor and for many of them, they are crestfallen. Shocked that the editor didn't embrace and agree with every nuance they had written.

Critiques may sting, but the information received can be helpful in making you a better writer. An author. Of course, the manner in which it is delivered makes a huge difference. I would love critics to be kind and instructive. Some are. It's a "fat chance" for most. I want to see your success with my words helping to guide your walk, no matter how challenging it is. Holding your feet to the fire of your coming perfection.

> *Imagine yourself sitting in your home as a successful author.*
>
> *What surrounds you?*
>
> *Do you have pictures and memories of successful book signings?*
>
> *Are there awards for numerous book contests?*
>
> *Framed reviews?*
>
> *Do you have notebooks or files that contain fan mail from readers?*

Is the check for your first book framed?

Many authors create a Book Wall of Fame.
What does yours look like?

Do you have a contact email database of your
fans so that you can alert them of "news"?

Your book starts in the incubator of your mind. Gestating is what you are doing. You will set rules for yourself … and for others as you walk. My friend and writing coach Anne Randolph reminds me to "write from my heart"— advice I've relished from my first book—I just didn't know it. Anne didn't come into my life until 15 years after I published my first book. Since then, I've had numerous writing prompt sessions with her. Each time, I'm reminded to be "present in the now" and "to get out of the way of the page—to let my pen lead and guide me" to where I'm going. She says,

You are freeing the spirit and letting what needs
to come through your subconscious, by ink,
erupt onto the page.

You may be wondering, *What the heck does that mean?* Anne has always encouraged me to get my notebook out, or the yellow pad. Not my computer. At least at first. Instead, let my hands connect with where my imagination is leading me through my heart.

I never know what will flow—sometimes my imagination takes me down wacky lanes. What I do know is that the process works … and then I'm ready to write and roll.

In the forty-plus years that I've been speaking, writing, and publishing, I've created my own set of "rules"—rules that have evolved for me to get done what I'm working on. Cherry-pick and use what talks to you. And I know you will come up with your own rules and strategies that will move you forward.

My rules for new projects start with pencil and paper, and lots of sticky notes in multiple colors. It's the way I begin. When I see how the sticky notes start to compile, my visualizing moves into high gear. When I see and feel the flow, I can transition to my computer and let my fingers fly. Watch out, keyboard!

My rules include reading … to keep on learning.

My rules are that I rarely read what I first write—just let it flow. Then, I will go back to it when my writing steam slows down.

My rules tell me to leave the nags and critics at the door— they are not welcome in my space … and in my mind.

My rules are to be present to me … to my topic … in the NOW. That means no editing, spell-check, fact-checking … yet. Just write—it's where my creativity is in play.

My rules are to write when I'm fresh—otherwise, my receptors aren't ready. I'm aa early morning person … but when my writing time is a full day, or a week, I write until I drop. My mind and body have been prepped for a 14 to 16-hour journey. Otherwise, my creative juices want to call for the 5 o'clock happy hour. John gets wine. I get hot chai. Unless I've transitioned to be the creative cook in the kitchen. Different skills are now at play.

My rules for both fiction and nonfiction are "get to the story"—get to the point. Dump the fillers and fluff. This is not high school where you must write an essay of so many words. Usually less is more.

My rules have a timer—whether it's a few hours or multiple blocks … as in days … of time. There is a beginning, middle, and end to it. Trust your body and mind to know them. And here's what the dessert is: often, awesome lines flow in as I wrap up a writing session.

My rules include reading … to keep on learning. I read others in my genre, and I devour books that others have said are a good read.

My rule is not to waste my time. If I don't think it is a good read after reading several pages, the book is closed and discarded. It's time to pass to someone else or place it in a giveaway box. I do the same thing with movies and TV-type streaming. If I'm not loving it, I click it off.

My rules include commitments to myself with dates.
Promises of when I will be ready to publish are put on
my calendar—AND my designer's calendar..

My rules include dating stuff. All those notes I've written
in my prep work get dated as I make them and put away
in its folder for later use. Sometimes I add the location
and time they were made.

Remember, your Author's Walk is all about figuring
out where you are headed. I promise you, there will be
inroads into it. Diversions will surface. A few stumblings
will be encountered. And new paths and directions will
land that are not even in your mindset as you read this.

... Yet.

twelve

Continuing Your Walk

Your **WORDS** and
your **VOICE** are essential.

As you continue **The Author's Walk** *…*
your walk … it is crucial to reflect on what
is within you and why it needs to be tasted,
chewed on, sometimes swallowed,
and sometimes spat out.

From the start of your walk, knowing the true inten-
tionality as to the **WHY** you are writing and your
desire to publish will keep you upright in the process. That,
coupled with the **WHO** you are writing and publishing for
will catapult you ahead of most authors.

Throughout your walk, your senses will work overtime.

- Your eyes will deliver an unlimited feast of visuals suggested by your words and phrases you choose.

- Your ears will tiptoe, dance, and jump on sounds to create a symphony—ranging from smooth and calming to a woven mass with dissonance shouting.

- Your taste buds will salivate over words, phrases, and sentences that emerge from your mind and fingers, and a sigh of satisfaction waffles through the air as the richness of them flow and a chapter is completed.

- Your touch on the keyboard as the words and ideas surge forth; or the flip of a switch to start narration as your mind and thoughts dictate … many times in a "fast" forward mode.

- Your nose will crinkle with pleasure as the richness of your words stream—a scene is executed that generates a smile across your face; and the final touch is added to the last chapter.

- A "yes" flows out of your mouth. You can smell the air … this is a winner.

And it reinforces how mighty you are. You, and your words … your ideas … your stories … your wisdom … and yes, your voice. All are needed. For some, they will be vital and life-changing …even lifesaving. For others, the escapism and pleasure they deliver fuels imaginations and provides entertainment.

With the thousands of authors I have worked with, self-doubt surfaces at some point. They ask:

> *Is my story good enough?*
> *Am I credible?*
> *Will anyone believe me?*
> *Am I wasting my time?*
> *What if my book is not perfect?*
> *Will I sell any books?*
> *What if I get criticized?*
> *What if I fail?*

The common dominator is fear and lack of confidence. It is part of the vulnerability of being an author. Your Author Walk is one step at a time—steps that can flow easily. Others find potholes and road bumps.

It is all part of your walk.

Please trust me when I say, "Your words and your voice have power."

And trust yourself when you say … when you think, "My words and my voice have power."

The Power of WORDS and VOICE ...
Your WORDS and VOICE

Without your **words** and your **voice**, history **can become** silent. Literature is dumbed down and disappears. Science reporting is crippled. Thought and speculation are at a standstill.

Without your **words** and your **voice**, the development and revealing of civilization would be impossible.

Without your **words** and your **voice**, the story-telling, the visuals, and the narratives of the imagination ebb to oblivion.

Without your **words** and your **voice**, the engines of change disappear ... windows that are the lighthouses erected in the sea of tides recede and vanish.

Without your **words** and your **voice**, the companions, the teachers, and the bankers of the mind fade away and cease to exist.

Without your **words** and your **voice**, innovative ideas and solutions will wither to invisibility.

Without your words and your voice, everyone is diminished.

Your *words* and your *voice* are essential.

Who are your words and voice for?

Why are you ready to share them?

Will you?

And *When*?

Author secret

for success:

trust your

journey ...

just get **started**.

Viva Voce

If **The Author's Walk** has encouraged you, inspired you, enlightened you, and given you hope, it's a Happy Dance for me.

And this is my Ask … share it with others. Word-of-mouth is what moves books. *Viva Voce.* Yours to your friends and to those you know that are thinking of writing. Or in the process of writing. Or another author who just might enjoy where I've come from on my walk. A walk that is now directing me to fiction.

Discover my website: *www.TheBookShepherd.com.* There's lots there to enhance your author success odds.

And why not … post a review on Amazon. *Viva Voce* in action … customer comments are read.

Thank you,

Judith

The Book Shepherd

Creating Successful Authors with Practical Publishing Guidance

Use your words ...

That's what matters.

Dr. Judith Briles is The Book Shepherd ... Publishing and Book Marketing Expert, Coach, Consultant, Podcaster ... and Author of 43 books. In addition to *The Author's Walk*, her main author success books include *How to Avoid Book Publishing Blunders, How to Create a Million Dollar Speech, How to Create Crowdfunding Success for Authors,* and *Snappy Sassy Salty Success for Authors*. Her memoir *When God Says NO* has received 14 book awards. In 2022, she published her historical fiction debut with co-author Brian Barnes, *The Secret Journey*.

Her podcast, *AuthorU-Your Guide to Book Publishing,* is heard globally with over 14 million downloads. She has been guest featured on more than 1500 print, radio, and TV programs.

Calling Colorado home, when she's not working with clients, you'll find her cooking, gardening, and entertaining friends.

Subscribe to her Tuesday / Saturday blogs and her Wednesday newsletter on her website, *https://TheBookShepherd.com.*

113

Books available for publishing help

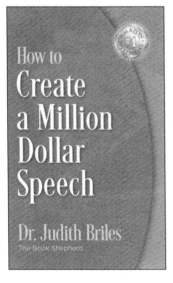

I'm Grateful ...

The Author's Walk is my 43rd book that carries my name on it. My hands, eyes, creativity, and spirit have been on countless others. Few projects are done on a solo basis. Mine are no exception. It takes a team—a village—to build and publish a book. And friends. I am grateful I have many of both.

Every Monday afternoon ... Ellen Tryon, Glenda Squire, and Mary Kobberstad join me for an hour of catchup at the end of the day for encouragement, ahas, insights, sometimes silliness, and sometimes reality check. They are my Heart Sisters. Thank you Ellen, Glenda, and Mary. I'm grateful for you just being you, and there.

Close friends who get and know "the grind" authors go through ... are essential in my mix. In the creative side. In the writing. In the marketing. In the thick and thin of authoring and publishing. Both Mara Purl and Susan RoAne have traveled a combined 70 years with me. Thank you, Mara and Susan. I'm grateful for your friendship and being able to call before dawn or late at night—sometimes just to hear your voice, ask for your opinion, get some help, or share something outrageous.

The creation of a book is impossible ... without a team to take ideas and turn them into images and graphics. To design pages that engage readers. To take the vision, voice, and the words of the author and magic wand them into a cover and interior that could never be called ho-hum. Rebecca Finkel did that for me ... again and again. And for our joint clients. Thank you, Rebecca. I'm grateful for your creativity.

Nick Zelinger is not only a skilled graphics pro, but has designed several of my books. Being able to bounce ideas off and with him when I'm working on my own clients as well as our joint clients is a gift. Thank you, Nick. I'm grateful for your "can-do" attitude and "does-do" results.

What author doesn't need tech and website help? … no one I know of. And when it comes to techie stuff along with gizmos and gadgets, Kelly Johnson steps up to the plate with the right bat. Thank you, Kelly. I'm grateful that you always have the answers or can lead me to where to find them.

Photos—authors need plenty of them … and no one has a better eye than Ashlee Bratton. It's a play date when she and her lens are at work. Thank you, Ashlee. I'm grateful for your keen eyes and imagination and I love the magic you capture.

Books have words … lots of them. And they need to have them added—deleted—adjusted and fine-tuned. For years, Peggie Ireland and Barb Wilson have read mine; felt mine; and red-lined them. For me. And for my clients. In the end, the manuscript that I thought was done … is finally done. Thank you, Peggie and Barb. I'm grateful for the input and willingness to stretch my writing and rewrites to new levels.

We authors need more hours in the day … many more hours. Without Leah Dasalla by my Skype side every morning, I wouldn't get done what I get done. Her 5:30 a.m. message each day: "What can I do for you today?" or "I need the marketing pushes for Saturday's program," or whatever, to her final message, "I'm shutting down in a few minutes. Is there anything you need from me?" are as essential as my first mug of tea. Thank you, Leah. I'm grateful for your loyalty, your commitment to what I do, and what you do for my author community.

Authors need juice in their lives ... my juice is the many thousands of authors I meet at conferences and events and my thousands of clients who have brought their manuscripts to me. Trusting that their words and finished book will shine. Thank you. I'm grateful and honored to work with you and support your dream to reality. And I'm grateful to join you on Your Author's Walk.

What we do ... accomplish ... deal with ... and get through ... wouldn't happen without others.

The village.

Indeed, gratefulness reigns supreme.

Pure author joy ...

when you know

that your chapter

is **the end** ... and

then your mind

and fingers start

the **next**.

Made in United States
North Haven, CT
05 March 2023

33614263R00072